LEARNING RESOURCES CENTER
UNIVERSITY OF WYOMING LIBRARIES
LARAMIE, WY 82071

WITHDRAWN

Living in
HONG KONG

Anthony Shang

Silver Burdett

Series editor: Belinda Hollyer
Book editor: John Morton
Series designer: Sally Boothroyd
Picture researcher: Suzanne Williams
Production controller: John Moulder

Consultant: Walter Easey
Teacher consultant: Cheung Siu Ming

Cover picture: Fisherfolk homes moored in front of crowded apartment blocks and factories. More and more of the people who live and work on these boats are abandoning their traditional way of life for jobs and homes on the land. Eventually, Hong Kong's floating villages will be just a picturesque memory.

Endpapers: Advertising signs clutter the space above a typical city street in Hong Kong. At night, these signs are a dazzling display of colored neon lights.

Title page: Outdoor sports or pastimes, such as rollerskating, are a popular way to escape from the tiny homes in which most Hong Kong people live.

Contents page: A senior citizen relaxes in a children's playground.

Artists
Dave Eaton: 44 (animals of Chinese calendar)
Gary Hincks: main map and area map 42-43
Martin Man: 12-13, 44 (Chinese characters)
Gary Rees: 42-43

Photographic sources

Key to position of pictures:
(T) top, (C) centre, (R) right, (L) left, (B) bottom

All photographs in this book were supplied by Sally and Richard Greenhill, with the exception of the following:

BBC Hulton Picture Library: 10B
Colorific/Ken Haas: 13T
Daily Telegraph Colour Library/A. Low: 40 B
Robert Harding Picture Library: 19, 20T
Hong Kong Government: 22C, 39B
Campix/Hutchison: 32-33T, 33B (photos Lesley Nelson)
OAPL/Kevin Phillips: 38B
Popperfoto: 11T
Rex Features Ltd: 10T, 26-27T
South China Morning Post: 40TL
ZEFA: Cover, 18, 20B, 32B, 33TR

A MACDONALD BOOK
© Macdonald & Company 1985
First published in Great Britain in 1985
by Macdonald & Company (Publishers) Ltd
London and Sydney
A member of BPCC plc
All rights reserved

Adapted and published in the
United States in 1986 by
Silver Burdett Company,
Morristown, N.J.

Library of Congress Cataloging in Publication Data

Shang, Anthony, 1952–
  Living in Hong Kong.

  (City life) (A Silver Burdett library selection)
  Bibliography: p.
  Includes index.
  Summary: Text and photographs depict various aspects of life in one of the world's most densely populated cities, including the floating villages, the shanty towns, the festivals, and traditions and culture preserved from the past.
  1. Hong Kong—Social life and customs—Juvenile literature.   [1. Hong Kong—Social life and customs] I. Title.   II. Series.
DS796.H75S42   1986   951'.2505   85-40306
ISBN 0-382-09115-9

Contents

A land and its people 8

From opium to industry 10

Living with the past 12

A city of the gods 14

Village Hong Kong 16

Lantau and the outer islands 18

The fisherfolk 20

Shanty towns 22

The Chans 24

Earning a living 26

Growing up in Hong Kong 28

Pastimes 30

Festivals 32

All-weather city 34

Getting around 36

Gateway to China 38

A place on borrowed time 40

Map of Hong Kong 42

Further information 44

Index 45

A land and its people

Few cities in the world can match Hong Kong's striking contrasts – on the one hand a neon-lit concrete jungle where money rules; on the other a thriving Chinese community, where ancient traditions survive, adapted to the 20th century.

Hong Kong has been a British colony since 1841. Today a few tiny communities of Europeans, and other Asians such as Indians and Filipinos, give the colony an international flavor. Yet from the chatter of voices to the distinctive cooking smells, Hong Kong is unmistakably Chinese.

City and country

As the jet makes its final approach to land at the airport in Kowloon, passengers see tall skyscrapers looming up from Hong Kong Island. But brightly-colored hillside temples are a reminder that Hong Kong is located on the southern tip of China.

The built-up city areas hugging Hong Kong Island's north shore are separated from urban Kowloon peninsula by a deep harbor. Indeed, Hong Kong's Chinese name, "Fragrant Harbor," aptly describes the perfect natural harbor of Asia's largest city port.

But these crowded areas only occupy a tiny fraction of the colony's land area. Hong Kong consists of 235 islands, big and small, and a large stretch of mainland called the New Territories. Since so much of the land is hilly, settlements are crammed together along flat land on the coast and in the valleys.

A crowded city

Hong Kong is one of the world's most crowded cities. Its population numbers about 5,500,000. Whether catching a bus or lining up for a movie, nobody can ignore the signs of a city bursting at its seams. Densely-packed slum blocks, high-rise apartments and factories surround the airport. Wooden shanty huts on the distant hillsides are a sad sign that housing is the city's major problem.

The earliest inhabitants

It was only after Hong Kong became a thriving British trading base that Chinese people began to arrive in large numbers.

Below: An old walled village, Tsang Tai Uk, in the New Territories. The Cantonese settled the fertile lowland areas; walled villages protected them from marauding pirates, bandits and clans who arrived later and had to make do with poor hilly land.

In the background are some of the apartments of Sha Tin, one of the new towns. Over 200,000 people live in Sha Tin but eventually it will house about 900,000 of Hong Kong's growing population.

Before then, Hong Kong was almost deserted. Apart from a few village people, the original inhabitants were Tanka or Hoklo people who lived on boats and fished for a living. Today their descendants huddle together in a few floating villages. Each year poverty forces more of them to give up their traditional life on water to seek jobs and homes on the land.

The ancestors of the Chinese people in Hong Kong came from different regions of China. The first to arrive, about a thousand years ago, were the Cantonese from southern China. Many were soldiers fleeing from the foreign Mongolian rulers in Peking; others were people who had lost their land. Most Cantonese people were related to each other through one male ancestor, and so belonged to the same clan. Naturally, the first clans to arrive built villages on the best land, in what is now called the New Territories.

Several hundred years later the first Hakka people arrived. Traditionally the Hakka were a wandering people, with no real home. In the past Hakka women were easily identified by their feet, for Hakkas were among the few Chinese groups who did not bind baby girls' feet. (Tiny feet were thought to be a sign of female beauty in Old China, and many families crippled their daughters by cramping their feet into tight bandages, which prevented normal growth. Even today, a few old women, born before the custom was banned, still hobble along on painfully deformed feet.)

Language problems

Today over half Hong Kong's people are under 24, and the majority of the population was born in the colony. But until recently, Hong Kong was a city of immigrants from various parts of China, where people who live in different regions speak local versions of Chinese. There are dozens of these local "dialects," and two people speaking different dialects cannot understand each other; for example, people in Canton say the word for "two" in the same way that people from Peking pronounce the word for "one." Written Chinese does not vary, so Hong Kong people read the same newspapers. But most people in the colony speak one of three dialects as their main language; someone who only understands Chiu Chao cannot converse with a Hakka speaker. However, today most people have learned to speak Cantonese, even if it's not their native language.

Above: Double-decker streetcars reflect British ways, but they are an ideal solution to public transportation on congested Hong Kong Island.

Below: A porter in her distinctive Hakka hat. Hakka women are often employed as laborers in Hong Kong, frequently on building sites.

From opium to industry

Tea and silk were sold for fortunes in 19th century Europe, and British merchants were eager to buy more of these luxuries from China. But they could offer little in return: as a Chinese emperor explained, "We possess all things in abundance, and have no need for the manufactures of outside Barbarians."

The Opium Wars

The merchants' solution was to sell opium to China. Opium is a dangerously addictive drug, made from poppies that grew in British India. China tried to ban the trade, but failed to stop thousands of its people from becoming addicts. Eventually, China's rulers were so alarmed at the cost and scale of opium imports that they confiscated drugs worth $2,500,000 from the dealers in Canton.

Outraged, the British occupied Hong Kong to give the dealers a safe base. By 1842 the colony officially belonged to Britain. More Chinese land was taken over the years until, in 1898, China was forced to lease a large area of land to Britain for 99 years. These "New Territories" completed Hong Kong's growth.

The coolie trade

Opium was not the only profitable trade. Slavery was ending and a new supply of cheap labor was needed. Contract laborers, called coolies, replaced the slaves. Many coolies had fled poverty and oppression in China. Chinese dealers met them in Hong Kong and, by persuading or kidnapping them, sold them to British merchants, who sent them to help build American railroads or work on West Indian and South American plantations. The coolies were treated cruelly, and kept in cages on the British ships. Public outrage at the high death rates on the journey eventually forced the government to ban the trade.

Right: Illegal immigrants from China try to reach Hong Kong by hiding in a sampan. Others swim from China or try to cross the land border. Until 1981, Hong Kong's "touch base" policy allowed immigrants who reached the city to stay in the colony. Pressure from China ended this. Now immigrants who are caught are sent back to China.

Below: An opium smoker. Rich Chinese smoked opium, but it was a welcome and pain-numbing relief to weary and hungry peasants. Today an even more dangerous drug – heroin – is made from opium poppies.

China's rulers were angry at having to waste their country's silver currency on "foreign mud" (their scornful term for the sticky, black opium). The humiliating treaties that followed the opium wars with Britain have left lasting resentment in China.

Life in 19th century Hong Kong

British governors tried to restrict Chinese people to the New Territories, because the Europeans did not want to mix with them. Chinese housing was appalling and some greedy landlords crammed as many as ten large families into one house, where people shared rooms with their pigs. Plague and malaria soon forced the Europeans to live on the main island's Peak District, where a cooler, less humid climate made life more pleasant and safer. For many years the Peak District was not only an exclusive all-white area, but also a symbol of success.

Refugees from China

From the 1860s onward, Chinese refugees crossed into Hong Kong as wars, peasant revolts, floods and drought ravaged the

mainland. Hong Kong was a haven to many Chinese people, who called it "a golden mountain, where men ate fat pork" (pork was a luxury for most Chinese peasants).

In 1937 Japan invaded China, and thousands of people fled to Hong Kong. But it was a brief escape – Japan invaded the colony in 1941. By 1945, with Japan's defeat and the end of World War II, Hong Kong was freed, but by then its population had fallen to 600,000.

In 1949 the Chinese civil war ended, and Hong Kong's population had risen to 2,000,000. The civil war had ranged since 1927, splitting China into Nationalist or Communist supporters. The Communist victory caused hundreds of thousands of Nationalists to cross into Hong Kong.

Disaster and recovery

Among the Nationalist refugees were wealthy Shanghai cotton mill owners, who arrived with money, machinery and many of their skilled workers. Their skills and enterprise began a new cloth-making industry in Hong Kong.

In 1950 war broke out between North and South Korea. China soon came to North Korea's aid, while the Western countries, including Britain, sided with the armies of the South. To prevent goods from reaching the North Korean armies the West banned all trade with China. (Until then trade with China had been vital to Hong Kong.) The ban left thousands jobless. But almost overnight, the new clothing industry came to the rescue, turning Hong Kong from a trader into a manufacturer. Other industries followed, and today Hong Kong is a thriving exporter of its own goods. Yet success has brought wealth to just a few people; for most people, Hong Kong's success has only come through hardship, long working hours and barely tolerable working and living conditions.

Below: A 1940's black and white photo, taken from Victoria Peak, of Hong Kong Island and the tip of Kowloon. In the mid 1960s the government (which owns all the land) allowed more offices to be built and began a property boom.

Some of the results of this can be seen in the color photo taken from the same point in 1984. The building with cranes on its roof is the new Hong Kong and Shanghai Bank.

Living with the past

Below: Most bodies are buried in temporary graves, while relatives look for a good *fung-shui* burial site that will bring them good luck. After seven years the bones are dug up for cleaning. This cemetery keeper does the job with respect, neatly laying out the bones and then carefully stacking them in an urn. The family keeps the urn until a final grave is found, often many years after the ancestor's death.

Because land is so expensive there are few cemeteries, and so cremation is becoming more common.

Chinese civilization was greatly influenced by Confucius, a teacher and philosopher who lived 2,500 years ago. He believed people should pay great respect to others, especially to their parents and grandparents. He thought that obedience, loyalty, kindness and correct behavior would create a peaceful, smooth-running society. Despite huge changes in the last century, many Chinese still retain the old ways and teach their children Confucian folktales and moral proverbs. In a city where life is tough, these teachings can reassure people.

Family loyalties

The ideas of Confucius still produce tightly-knit families. Toddlers are adored and rarely spanked. But as they grow up, children are taught to respect their parents – especially their fathers. Even if parents seem harsh and unfair, children must learn to obey them.

Such ideas give men an unfair advantage over women: attitudes are changing (especially in the city), but a son's birth is still celebrated by decorating a house with lanterns and lucky posters. Sons represent security and are expected to look after their aging parents, for pensions and unemployment or sickness benefits are rare.

Ancestor worship

Children also learn respect for their dead ancestors. Ancestor worship is the way a family honors an ancestor's achievements in life.

Traditionally, a dead person gets the best funeral a family can afford. Relatives grieve in white or beige gowns. Rich families hire mourners for extra tears, and musicians to play cymbals, gongs and wind instruments.

A traditional red marriage

Having children, especially a son to carry on the family name, is a couple's first ancestral duty. Arranged marriages (which still happen in the villages) reflect this. A matchmaker, often a female friend or relative, is asked by parents to find a partner for a son or daughter. Then a fortune-teller checks the precise times of the couple's birthdays, though it is the parents who make the final decision. If all is well, an engagement is announced and gifts are made to the girl's family.

Red is lucky, so it is a favorite choice for weddings. The bride's dress is red and the

Below: Choosing a good grave site is very important and there are strict *fung-shui* rules to be followed. It is essential that the grave of the dead relative should have a view of the sea or at least of a pleasant valley and that the site should be open to fresh breezes. This means that cemeteries often occupy natural or man-made hillsides. Families gather at their ancestors' graves at special festivals to make offerings and ask for good fortune in any new ventures.

groom has a red sash, while women wear red threads in their hair. The bride travels to the wedding in a sedan chair carried by four of the groom's family. Her journey symbolizes the leaving of her own family for her husband's. Tradition expects her to serve and obey her new mother-in-law. In cities and many villages, cars now replace sedan chairs.

Matchmaking is rare in the city, and couples meet at work or through friends. Discos are expensive, but the beach is an ideal meeting place, even though a boy and girl seldom go alone the first time. Most people choose whom they marry, but they still like to get their parents' consent.

Cosmic *fung-shui*

For centuries Chinese life has been influenced by a belief in the power of natural forces, or *fung-shui*. Used well, they help people; if ignored, they bring disaster.

Even the government and large companies respect these powers; *fung-shui* experts were hired to ensure the success of the costly Mass Transit Railway.

According to the rules, buildings must face south, and no road or path may lead straight to the door, for this invites evil spirits. Usually, though, people must make a compromise and weigh good factors against the bad – sites are rarely perfect.

Get it while you can

Hong Kong society encourages many people to see making a lot of money as the most important thing in life. Younger Chinese people tend to be particularly influenced by this. Those who do make fortunes are proud to show their success by using costly foreign luxuries, such as expensive French brandy.

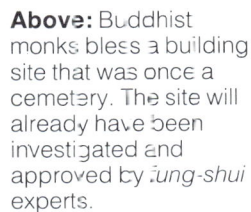

Above: Buddhist monks bless a building site that was once a cemetery. The site will already have been investigated and approved by *fung-shui* experts.

Left: A couple wants to buy this apartment, so they have hired a geomancer. In his left hand he holds a *fung-shui* compass, whose eight points represent the natural elements – fire, heaven, wind, the sea, thunder, hills, earth, and rain. In his right hand is a site plan of the apartments.

Fung-shui is complex, but one thing to guard against is water flowing away from the main window; a stream or a drain could be bad luck.

Left: Many Hong Kong Chinese maintain a tradition of regularly taking the whole family out to a restaurant on Sunday mornings. They have a special dish called *dim-sum* which are savory dumplings that are steamed and served from round bamboo baskets. There are as many as sixty different varieties to choose from. They are wheeled to the table on a trolley and the person serving will often chant a rhyme or proverb for each one.

A city of the gods

Worship is a daily event for many Hong Kong people. Praying is a personal affair; there are no special days for worship or priests to take services. Even when people pray aloud together, they seldom use the same prayer.

Different gods for different needs
The Chinese in Hong Kong have scores of gods from whom they seek help, at different times and for different reasons. No profession or trade is without its own god. For example, Man (the God of Literature) is honored by civil servants and journalists. Temples are named after gods, and the God of War (Mo) and the God of Literature share Man Mo temple.

Different human needs are looked after by various gods. Wong Tai Sin brings good luck and good health, so sick people and gamblers seeking horse-racing tips often pray to him.

The gods are important in the "other world." Many Chinese believe that when they die, they will go before ten Judges of the Underworld, who punish evil people.

Popular religions
Most Chinese gods stem from two ancient religions – Taoism and Buddhism. Taoism

Below: A police station shrine to the God of War, who is also worshiped by gangsters.

teaches people to live a peaceful life in harmony with nature. There are hundreds of Taoist gods, who are either legendary figures or real people who achieved fame during their lives.

Many gods are believed to have powers which ensure good harvests or cure illness. The most popular god is Tin Hau (Queen of Heaven), who is thought to control the sea and weather. Given the colony's links with the sea, Hong Kong has over 25 Tin Hau temples. Tin Hau protects fisherfolk, and sailors often visit one of her temples to make prayers and offerings for a safe voyage.

Buddhism encourages people to seek an understanding of themselves and the world they live in. This understanding is called "enlightenment." Buddhism is followed in many parts of Asia, but Chinese Buddhists have their own gods. One of them, Koon Yum (the Goddess of Mercy), is said to end suffering and bring enlightenment with one tender glance.

Temples and festivals
Most Hong Kong festivals and public holidays involve religious worship, and the colony has over 500 temples named after Buddhist or Taoist gods. Temples are usually located in the best *fung-shui* sites, ideally on hill-slopes facing the sea, and are easily recognizable by their bright colors.

The Monkey God's temple is popular with children. This god is said to have begun as a stone monkey, who was taught magic tricks by a Taoist priest. When the monkey began to alter his appearance and jump between clouds, he became such a nuisance that he was banished to a remote part of China.

Practical matters
People have a very practical approach to their religion: they consult their gods on such matters as career prospects or lucky dates. Most people cannot say if the gods they pray to are Buddhist or Taoist. Nor do they observe all the religious rules. Taoist and Buddhist laws strictly forbid the killing of animals for food, yet the Chinese do not hesitate to eat meat – they even make meat offerings to the gods!

Right: A palmist and a face-reader near Wong Tai Sin temple. Fortune-tellers often dress traditionally, for this attracts customers.

Left: Incense coils hang from the roof of Man Mo temple. Most incense is made in thin sticks, and plays an important part in worship. The urn on the right glows with burning paper offerings.

Above: Women at Wong Tai Sin temple shake oracle stick holders. When a stick falls out, they note its number, whose meaning is listed in the ancient "Book of Changes." For a fee a soothsayer will explain a number's message to a worshiper.
The temple pillars are painted red for happiness. The roof is gold for wealth.

Left: Paper money (and goods like cars or planes) is burned in the belief that it will pass into the possession of the dead in their afterlife.

Temples are run as businesses, and temple keepers earn a living by selling joss sticks and paper offerings. Some charge admission fees while others rely on donations. Outside a temple there are many services to meet worshipers' needs, such as stalls selling paper money and offerings. There is an alley of stalls by Wong Tai Sin temple, where soothsayers and palmists tell the future or help to answer people's prayers.

A city of many faiths

There are small groups of Muslims, Jews and Sikhs in Hong Kong. There are also over 500,000 Christians and more than 850 Christian churches. In many villages the church is the best-kept building. Some Chinese Christians originally converted to obtain welfare aid from Christian charities, or to get their children into church schools.

Village Hong Kong

Every day at 6 p.m. Tang Wong Hing finishes his overtime at the watch factory in industrial Kowloon. He then makes the long journey by Mass Transit Rail and bus to his village, Ping Shan, in the New Territories. Mr Tang is one of the few people who works in the city but still lives in a village.

Cantonese villages

Most of the people who live in Mr Tang's village share the same surname. They are all relatives – clanspeople sharing one male ancestor. Clans are male-dominated, and women gain "associate" membership in their husbands' clans only by marriage. The Tang clan is one of the five great Cantonese clans in the New Territories; the others are Pang, Hau, Liu, and Man clans.

Right: An ancestral hall decorated for a festival; a special time to worship ancestors. Inside is an altar, with the ancestors' names above it. Many Chinese believe that when their parents die, their spirits remain to help their children. In return, the living have a duty to make offerings to their dead ancestors. When parents die, their own ancestral duties pass on to their children. In this way, the living have duties to their parents, their parents' parents, and even further back.

Hakka newcomers

The Hakkas are the poor farmers, who had to settle for the less fertile land on the hills and rugged areas of the eastern side of the New Territories. On some hilly outer islands, Hakka farmers have scraped a living from the land for centuries.

Hakka villages are usually smaller than Cantonese ones, with fewer grand buildings. Many villagers have different surnames, though families with the same surname, such as Wong, usually live in one part of the village. Women, traditionally dressed in black pajama suits and black-rimmed hats, do most of the farm work in Hakka villages.

Above: Poultry on their way to a city market. Chicken, ducks, geese, pigeons and even quail are all a valuable source of income for farmers in the New Territories.

Left: Fish breeding in ponds is very profitable. Farmers do not just breed edible fish, like varieties of carp, but also goldfish, which make ideal pets in tiny city apartments. On the coast, farmers also breed marine fish.

Rivalries

Cantonese and Hakka countryfolk have never got along together, and in the past disputes led to feuds and bloody fights. Squabbles between neighboring villagers still arise over the use of irrigation pumps or over land borders. Rural Hakkas are often superstitious, and if their shrines to local gods are damaged, they will probably blame the Cantonese.

In the old days, villages were raided for livestock and other valuables by marauding pirates or other villagers. Wealthy Cantonese built walls around their villages to protect themselves from their neighbors. The best preserved walled village is Kat Hing Wai,

Below: A tenant farmer irrigates his land with a traditional water scoop. Fresh water has always been scarce in Hong Kong, and it was often a source of argument in the past. Today, during a drought, water supplies to homes all over Hong Kong are cut off. People may go without water for as long as 14 hours a day.

Even though reservoirs have been built, Hong Kong still imports about half its water from China.

In villages like Ping Shan toddlers are tended by old women, who chat in alleys while old men sit in tea-houses, talking and playing cards. Senior clansmen and rich farmers form councils to decide village affairs. At night a watchman beats his drum every hour on his rounds.

But life is changing fast as the 20th century overtakes the villages. Huge new towns and industrial estates compete with the villages for land. Color televisions, video machines and Japanese cars are common. Empty houses are used as workshops, where foods such as Chinese smoked sausages are made for sale in the city markets.

Some of the richest villages are those where most able-bodied men have left to work in Chinese restaurants in other parts of the world. They regularly send back money to support elderly relatives. In fact, most Chinese people who emigrated in the 1950s and 1960s came from New Territories villages.

which is surrounded by a fifteen-foot thick wall and a 500-year-old moat.

Farming: a dying occupation

Up to the 1950s, farming was the main income for villagers like the Tangs. Rural life followed the planting, harvesting and threshing of two rice crops a year. Today, paddy fields are rare. Rice output has fallen dramatically since the 1950s, in competition with cheap Thai and Chinese rice. Hong Kong now imports most of its food; almost all by train and ship from China.

Only 9% of Hong Kong's land is fit to farm. Cantonese landowners find it more profitable to rent their fields to Hakka tenant farmers and to newly arrived refugees. Instead of rice, most farmers grow more valuable crops such as watercress, cabbages, tomatoes, gourds, spring onions and long beans. Fruits like lychees, lemons, tangerines and guavas grow on the hill slopes. Other farmers keep pigs and poultry, or rear fish in ponds.

Village life today

Traditional buildings with low clay-tiled roofs still survive in the New Territories; some roofs have carved decorations on their straight or curved ridges. The most attractive buildings are the temples and ancestral halls. Most halls belong to Cantonese clans who worship their ancestors there.

Below: Hakka women pose in traditional costume for tourist photographers. They charge a few dollars, and it's useful extra income. Some have even been able to give up farm work and support themselves in this way.

Lantau and the outer islands

No description of Hong Kong is complete without mentioning its islands. Few visitors know the islands, for they are hard to reach. Except for the bigger ones like Lantau, Cheung Chau and Lamma, which have regular ferry links, most of them are small, and can only be reached by private boat.

Few people live on the islands today, and many are uninhabited. Although the islands are almost empty and the cities are overcrowded, people need to be able to get to work easily. Since more jobs are in the cities, most people have little choice about where they live.

Traditional crafts
Because the islands are so isolated, they seem almost untouched by the 20th century. Electricity and piped water supplies are rare, because it is too expensive to supply just a few homes. Some islanders still cook on clay stoves, and live chickens are often kept in kitchens.

Many people work at traditional crafts, using ancient skills passed on from family to family over many generations. Old-fashioned junks are built on wooden slipways on the beaches. Although the boats may have engines, there are still traditional sail makers. When a junk is ready for launching, fragrant-smelling incense is burned in honor of Tin Hau, the fisherfolk's god.

Even the incense is made on the islands. Locally-grown bamboo is split into thin sticks. These are dipped into a mixture of incense powder (powdered wood), sawdust (which helps the sticks to burn), and strong-smelling substances like sandalwood or rose powder. After coating, the sticks are spread outside to dry. During the rainy season, when the air is damp, this can take all day. Fatter sticks may need several drying sessions.

Noodles are also dried in the sun. When the noodle maker has kneaded and stretched the dough until it is smooth and elastic, it is cut into strips, and hung on bamboo poles to dry.

Lantau, island of prayer
Lantau is by far the largest island. Twice the size of Hong Kong Island, it has only 15,000

Right: Traditional fisherfolk at work in the quiet waters surrounding one of Hong Kong's many islands.

Recent discoveries of ancient pottery and stone tools suggest that some islands were inhabited over 5,000 years ago. These prehistoric people may have been the first people to live and fish in the area. Today, it is thought, the descendants of these people live in Vietnam.

Right: Po Lin monastery was founded in 1905. Although the traditional Chinese building looks very old, it was actually built in 1970.

The carved animals at the corners of the roof serve to remind Buddhists that they are not supposed to kill animals. Visitors to the monastery and its beautiful gardens can eat special Buddhist vegetarian meals at the monastery restaurant. Po Lin also provides rooms for people who wish to spend a night away from the noisy bustle of the cities.

inhabitants – one hundredth of the main island's population.

Lantau's peaceful countryside provides a perfect atmosphere for nuns and monks to devote themselves to prayer and a religious life. As well as a few Christian monasteries, Lantau has 135 Buddhist monasteries; Po Lin (which means Precious Lotus) is the most famous. About 100 nuns and monks live here while men and women from neighboring countries come to train for a religious life. Po Lin is also home for some of Hong Kong's old people who have nowhere else to live. In return for helping in the kitchen or garden, elderly people are given a bed and food.

Ghost villages

The islands' unspoiled beaches and beautiful countryside attract city holidaymakers on weekends. But there are very few jobs for the local people. As older islanders die, and younger ones move to the cities, they leave behind "ghost villages" of deserted houses.

But there are plans that will stop this, at least on Lantau. Overcrowding in the cities has forced the government to consider building a bridge from Kowloon to northern Lantau. This would enable factories, housing developments, a new container port, and a power station to be built on the island, thus providing work to keep many people there. A bridge would also make it easier for tourists to visit Lantau. More than 2,500,000 tourists already visit Hong Kong each year, and if hotels, golf courses and shopping centers are built on the island, more tourists could spend longer holidays by the sea. These plans could also disrupt Lantau's peaceful way of life.

The fisherfolk

Hong Kong's Chinese seafood delicacies are famous: even a year's stay is not long enough to try every dish. Steamed or braised fish are popular, and the fish are often served complete with head and tail – the tail is thought to be very tasty, so everyone wants it! It is bad luck to turn a fish over on a plate in case it causes a boat at sea to capsize. Diners try to reach the flesh underneath without turning the fish over. This takes great skill with a pair of chopsticks!

Over 150 types of fish, including garoupa, pike, shark, sea bream and pomfret, live in the waters around Hong Kong. Freshwater fish, like carp and grey mullet, are bred in fish farms.

Fishing people and fishing villages

Most fish are caught by Hoklo or Tanka people. About 2,000 years ago, some Tanka rebels, so one story says, were banished from the land by the emperor and forced to live from the sea.

The Hoklo people fish in shallow waters, specializing in mussels, pilchards, oysters and herring. The Tanka own most deep sea trawlers and junks.

Although there are Hoklo fishing villages on islands like Lamma and Lantau, most fisherfolk cluster in the coastal havens of Aberdeen, Shau Kei Wan and Tai Po. About 70,000 people, mainly Tanka, still live on boats. But mechanization and China's

Left: Fish and shellfish are sold live, so as to be absolutely fresh.

Below: Aberdeen, Hong Kong's largest floating village. The huge red boat is a tourist seafood restaurant, where diners choose live fish from tanks, and have them cooked to order.

Above: Lui Heng's best friend plays with her yo-yo. The silver tank at the end of the boat contains gas for cooking and heating.

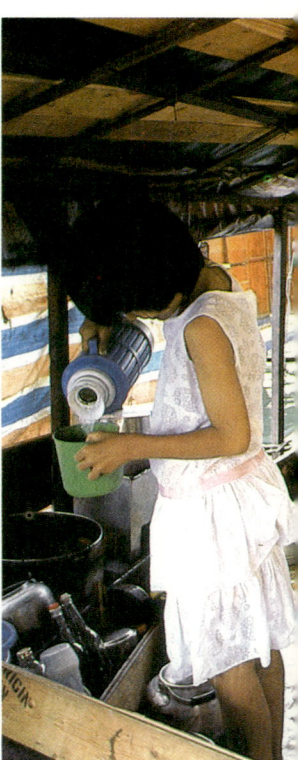

increased territorial fishing rights challenge the old ways. Deep sea trawlers, with small crews, sail out farther and make bigger catches in almost any weather than the small, traditional boats. Each year, more fisherfolk are unable to survive by fishing, and are driven to seek jobs on the land.

The Sheks' boat

Aberdeen may give a romantic view of life afloat. But for people like the Sheks, life on a boat is uncomfortable and hard work.

Mr. and Mrs. Shek and their six children live on a 20 year-old wooden boat built by Mr. Shek's cousin; he had no paper plans, just what his father taught him. The deck, 33 feet square, is the living area. While Mrs. Shek and her elder daughter make dinner, Mr. Shek plays cards or watches television. Lui Heng, the younger daughter, always complains that it's too noisy for homework.

Except for a chest of drawers and a small table, there's no room for furniture; a fold-up bed doubles as a sofa. There is no closet, so clothes hang everywhere.

The family sleeps in the stern cabin. Its ceiling is one yard high, so everyone has to crawl into bed. In the summer, Mr. Shek and his elder son sleep on deck – its's cooler than the stuffy cabin. A timber frame covered by a tarpaulin shelters them from the rain.

Everything the Sheks need comes from sampan "shops," which sail the busy waters once or twice a week. Floating grocers sell food and oil, and they can even get a haircut on a boat. When one son broke his ankle, it was bandaged up on a boat clinic.

The eldest children went to a floating primary school, but now they attend a shore school run by the Fish Marketing Organization. As the Shek's boat is near the shore, reaching the jetty is just a matter of hopping across a few decks.

Coming ashore

Mr Shek no longer fishes – he can't compete with modern diesel trawlers. Now he's an attendant at the Oceanarium on Hong Kong Island, and his pay has more than doubled. Soon he'll sell the boat, and the family will move to a fisherfolk housing development with fresh water on tap and electricity.

A few fisherfolk smuggle color televisions and other valuables to the Chinese coast; occasionally, they bring back illegal immigrants in their boats. Some run their boats as restaurants – tourists are paddled out to the boat. Other sampans provide fresh food and drink, and dinner is cooked and served on the tiny deck.

Left: The Sheks have to fetch water from a tap on the land, though it can also be bought from sampans. Water for drinking is boiled, and kept in thermos flasks. The bedroom is immediately behind Mr. Shek and the boys.

Below: The Sheks have no room for a large table, so they use the floor as a dining table. The main course of the meal is fish.

Shanty towns

It is hard to imagine a modern city where one in every eight people lives in huts built of scrap material. But illegal shanty towns spring up all over Hong Kong, wherever there is a bare hillside or some empty land. The shanty town squatters are ordinary working people who are not particularly poor. They eat and dress well and can afford a few luxuries, such as television sets. But they cannot afford private housing, and they are at the bottom of the public housing list.

A squatter's life
Electricity, proper sewers and tap water are luxuries for a squatter. Water for drinking, cooking and washing comes from taps

Above: Potted plants help soften the bleakness of a shanty town. Some squatters install air-conditioners, for a tin-roofed hut can be unbearably hot in summer.

In the background is a government housing complex, where most squatters hope to be rehoused one day.

Above: Fire is always a danger in shanty towns.

Right: Shanties are often built where no one else wants to build. Typhoon floods rushing down the steep slopes can easily wash away these flimsy homes.

outside; there are always long bucket lines. Lavatories, often wooden shacks, are shared by hundreds. Young children may be tempted to play in the filthy open sewers that cut through shanty towns.

Early squatters were refused proper supplies by the electricity company. People solved this problem by illegally tapping supplies from nearby shops. Even with a legal supply, a hut will be dimly lit because the voltage is kept low, so as to reduce the fire risk.

Huts with corrugated-iron roofs over timber-framed cardboard walls are very flimsy. A tiny shack often houses six or more people, who have to be extremely considerate to get on with each other without arguments. Inside it's surprisingly clean, for the squatters try to keep what dignity they can in such conditions.

Disaster and rehousing

Shanties are dangerous. Heavy rains leak in, and every year vicious typhoon winds reduce the huts to splinters. Fire is the worst fear; after one left 60,000 homeless in 1953, the government had to build the first public housing – the Phase I apartment blocks.

Over 650,000 squatters – who have no rights to their homes – live on government land. Every so often, government patrols raid their settlements and demolish the huts. When the government wishes to build on land occupied by squatters, or if there is a major disaster, squatters are rehoused – often on temporary sites. Here, a squatter is given a strictly-measured concrete plot for a floor (often smaller than the old shanty) and a little money to build an asbestos-roofed hut. Proper electricity and water supplies make this the first step towards decent housing.

Right: A Temporary Resettlement Area. The chalked sign on the wall indicates the floor space the family has been allocated. If a family builds a hut that is larger than this area, it will be pulled down by government officers.

Left: Squatter children contribute to their family's income by making furry toys.
Although this settlement is illegal, the government has erected parking meters on the right hand side of the road. Television aerials sprout from the roofs, and you can see illegal electricity cables on the far left.

The Chans

Mr. and Mrs. Chan live with three daughters and three sons in a one-room apartment, measuring fourteen by ten feet. They have been there since 1956, when the government moved them out of a Kowloon shanty town and into public housing in Tsuen Wan, one of Hong Kong's huge new towns.

To reach their bathroom they go outside, and down to the end of the communal corridor, where each family has its own numbered bathroom. Even though it's tiny, the Chans are lucky with their home; friends who live in an earlier building share a communal washroom with several hundred other people from their floor.

Mrs. Chan's kitchen
Every evening Mrs. Chan cooks dinner in the outside corridor. In the humid summer, her cooking turns the apartment into a steam bath. Any cool breezes are usually blocked by washing hanging over the corridor.

On Saturday nights, the Chans usually watch television or play Mah Jong – the noise of plastic Mah Jong tiles clacking on tables is a familiar sound all over Hong Kong.

Paul tries to go out on Saturdays, but if he stays in he spends hours phoning his girlfriend. The noise in the apartment makes

Above: Mrs. Chan serves beef and green peppers in black bean sauce. Her kitchen is a lock-up aluminium box with a gas stove, pots, pans and cutlery.

Left: The bathroom, where Mrs. Chan gets water for cooking. It's also where the Chans wash-up and keep a top-loading washing machine. There's no bath or shower, so the Chans wash themselves with buckets of water.

Every morning there's a rush for the bathroom. Paul (at 27, the eldest son) and Kum Fa and Kum Lin, the eldest daughters, are in a hurry to get to work.

Below: Part of Tsuen Wan, one of the huge industrial towns in the New Territories. The Chan's apartment is marked with a red ring.

Above: Uncle Wong has come to dinner. He bought roast pork and duck in a nearby shop, to add to Mrs. Chan's soup, shrimp omelette, and beef.

Below: Saturday night is Mah Jong night. Paul watches television and Bobby is phoning. Kum Yi gets ready to meet her boyfriend. Peter, above the divider, is trying to study.

An ancestor's photo is on the divider wall.

homework hard for young Bobby and Peter, who often go outside to study under the nearest quiet lamppost. At exam-time, they may study in the airport lounge. It's noisy there, but there's plenty of room, and it doesn't matter if it rains.

Bedtime
Preparing for bed takes a lot of organization. The room is divided in two by a cloth curtain covering the partition door – one bedroom for the men and one for the women. A cough or a restless sleeper wakes everyone up: when Bobby was a baby and cried at night, nobody slept properly.

The Chans at work
The Chans are not rich, but they are not poor. With four incomes, they can afford a few luxuries and even an air-conditioner, which is a blessing in summer. Paul is a packer at Kwai Chung container terminal just down the road, and Kum Lin is an infant teacher. Kum Fa has just been promoted to overseer in the garment factory where she works.

Mrs. Chan retired this year from helping in a camera factory canteen. In those days she kneaded dumpling dough at home to sell to the canteen, and the apartment was even more cluttered.

Mr. Chan is an assistant foreman on a building site. His wife worries that he might fall off the flimsy bamboo scaffolding. She tries to make him wear a helmet, but he often forgets. Everyone knows many accidents happen on the sites, but Mr. Chan has little time to worry about safety precautions. But he does wonder about the perfectly sound buildings he helps to demolish, especially when his boss replaces them with luxury apartments and offices. While the public housing lists grow longer, people like Mr. Chan's boss earn fortunes charging expensive rents for their properties.

More room for the Chans?
Mr. Chan often grumbles about the apartment, and dreams of a bigger one. But the rent would be too high, and he could never afford to buy one. Anyway, Kum Lin will marry her childhood sweetheart next year, Kum Fa is also engaged, and there will be more room when they both move out.

Like the Chans, nearly half Hong Kong's people live in public housing. But more is needed, and "mini-cities" like Sha Tin or Tai Po, are still growing. By 1990, they will have to house another 2,000,000 people.

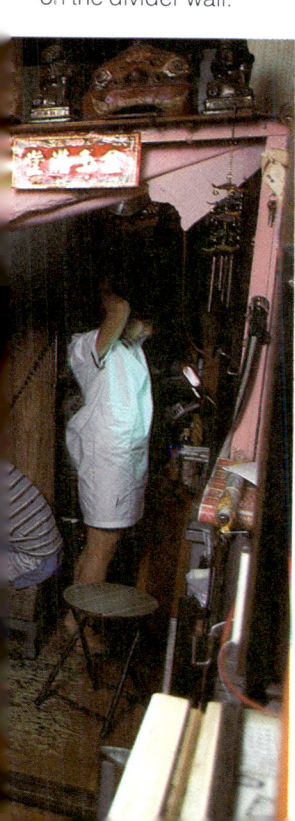

Left: Getting ready for bed. On the women's side there's a bunk bed. Mrs. Chan and 17 year-old Kum Yi share the bottom double part, while Kum Lin has the top single part. Finally, when the other three are in bed, Kum Fa sets up her folding bed beside her mother.

Mr. Chan and the sons all sleep on folding beds which they set up in the other half of the room.

Earning a living

Saturday in Hong Kong is a working day, with business as usual for factories and shops. Even banks and offices open for part of the day. People often work a ten-hour day, seven days a week. Hard work is a necessity. People need all they can earn to feed large families and save for the future; Hong Kong has no state pensions or unemployment benefits. People are expected to look after themselves in times of trouble and to provide for their elderly parents.

From warehouse to factory

Hong Kong began by trading in other countries' goods. Today, hard work and an ability to respond to new challenges have turned Hong Kong into a major manufacturer and exporter of a wide variety of goods.

Although many industries are found in the new towns, small factories operate in any available space. Empty houses are used to produce anything from plastic toys to car radios, while apartments may become tiny garment factories.

The textile industry is still the largest employer, producing woven cloth and garments like blouses, T-shirts, jeans and sweaters. Traditionally, Hong Kong's success has been based on low wages, and many workers are paid according to how many items they produce. A pair of jeans sold in an American shop for $30.00 was probably

Below: Most jeans are made with simple machines and a lot of hand work. The cloth is usually cut elsewhere, and sent to small workshops to be made up. Cloth cutting is skilled handwork.

Far right: a factory where cloth is cut with the aid of a computer. The computer makes a paper pattern, which is then used to guide a tool to cut dozens of pieces of cloth all at the same time.

Below: A rattanware furniture workshop. Rattanware is made from long stems of palm cane.

Most Hong Kong companies are small, with under 50 workers; workshops like this one are extremely common. They are often family concerns and employ few people outside the family. Many businesses produce their goods with little except raw materials, a few simple tools and human skill. If they find their products are no longer selling well, they can easily change to something else. If they used complicated machinery, it would be expensive and slow to alter their products.

Above: Boys at work in a light engineering workshop on the ground floor of a government housing project. Despite laws to stop children under 15 from working in factories, some employers openly break the law and employ children in their spare time from school.

bought from a Hong Kong factory for $4.00. Although workers specialize in making pockets, or sewing on zippers, the workers' share of the $4.00 would be about $1.50. But wages are rising, and other Far East countries can now undercut Hong Kong prices. One response to this has been an increasing use of advanced technology to make high quality goods. In some factories skilled jobs, like embroidery, are now controlled by computers. Other factories are making expensive fashion clothes like furs or silk dresses. They are designed in Europe or America, and are labeled with such famous fashion house names as Christian Dior or Fiorucci.

Factories making electrical goods such as fans or vacuum cleaners are common, but Hong Kong is also an important electronics assembly center. Spacious air-conditioned factories produce calculators, radios, digital watches and more sophisticated items such as telephone head-sets, desk computers and video games. Women assemble the parts, for they are said to have more nimble fingers. Using powerful microscopes all day to see the parts eventually damages their eyesight.

Rich and poor

In the last 15 years, the government has tried to improve Hong Kong's "sweatshop" image. Employers must now provide sick pay and at least seven days' paid vacation, and newer purpose-built factories are safer to work in. Compulsory education to the age of 15 has reduced child labor, and higher wages allow workers to buy a few luxuries such as color television sets and video recorders.

For its size, Hong Kong has more millionaires than any other country: the number of Mercedes Benz and Rolls Royce cars is startling proof of this. Yet the "rags to riches" dream of a poor refugee becoming a millionaire is less likely to come true today.

Offices and ancient crafts

Under half of Hong Kong's workers have factory jobs. Many others are employed in offices, banks and the civil service, while about 90,000 people in the building industry help satisfy a constant demand for new buildings.

Tourists are fascinated by Hong Kong's seemingly endless number of shops. The narrow streets of the Western District of Hong Kong Island are full of traditional craft workers such as jade or ivory carvers, goldsmiths, rattan furniture-makers or herbalists. Many tourists have a suit made to measure in 24 hours, at one of the hundreds of Indian or Chinese tailor shops. In a Kowloon parking lot, professional calligraphers will write letters in Chinese for old and illiterate customers.

Another reminder of the past are the "amahs" (domestic servants) who still work for rich families. Most amahs are fairly old, as younger women prefer the freedom of better-paying office or factory work.

Growing up in Hong Kong

All children go to school from the age of six to fifteen. But in the morning, only half of them set off to school! By lunch, school is over for them. The other half are not playing truant; their turn comes in the afternoon. Because of a shortage of places, many schools run morning and afternoon shifts. Even so, many classes have as many as 50 children.

A good education can be a passport to success for a poor person, and school is free up to the age of 15. Some children must work in the family business in their spare time. Traditionally, sons were always encouraged to study; old clan study halls are still found in the New Territories. Girls were not so lucky; their education was considered a luxury.

Classrooms

Class discipline is very strict. Pupils are expected to be attentively obedient, and to greet a teacher politely before each lesson. This was traditionally accepted in China, but Hong Kong schools often need to enforce it with punishment.

Lessons are taught from a blackboard, and children learn most things by constantly repeating them.

A colonial education

Children learn a lot about England, but that is hardly useful to Hong Kong's Chinese children, especially when they reach secondary school. They memorize passages from Shakespeare's plays, and English history. Until recently, math was taught using English pounds and pence rather than Hong Kong dollars and cents.

Competition to get into a good school is intense. Even toddlers take exams for nursery schools that may lead them to good primary schools. Rich children are often helped by private teachers, in the race for a university place. Hong Kong's two universities do not have enough places to go round, and even well-qualified students may fail to gain entry.

A pause for fun

Children can relax when they are not studying or helping their parents. Swimming on the beach is a favorite escape from cramped high-rise homes. Sports are popular, especially table-tennis, though you may have to wait hours for a game. Ten-pin bowling, ice skating and go-carting are popular but expensive.

Hong Kong's two film studios make many "kung-fu," comedy and thriller movies. Though home videos are common, young people love the excitement of the movies.

Other children prefer quiet street bookshops where they can sit on stools and read short stories or comics. For a small fee, books can be borrowed and taken home.

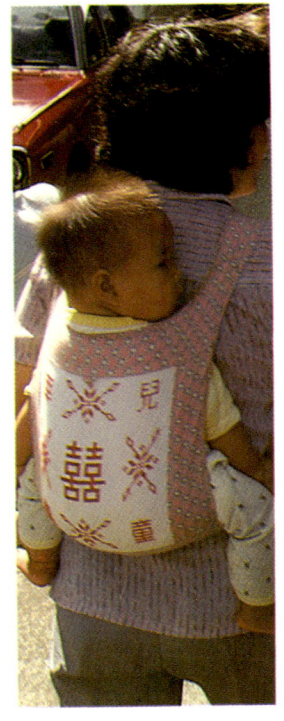

Above: The traditional way to carry babies. The writing on the baby's carrier means "children are happiness."

Below and right: Like young people anywhere, Hong Kong children will always find games to play in a street.

Left: A six year-old neatly copies "elder sister" in Chinese, until she knows the correct size and order of brush strokes. Children are taught written Chinese from their first day at school.

Western people often learn spoken Chinese, but few can write it. Chinese calligraphy is an art in itself.

Right: Junior lessons are usually in Chinese, but secondary children are mainly taught in English, and it is very difficult to have to learn a new language. Model English handwriting in traditional "copperplate" style has been painted on the blackboard. Chinese is spoken at home, but English is essential for a good job in a bank or the civil service.

The paper dragon on the wall is a class project for the Dragon Boat Festival in summer.

Left: Classrooms are neat and orderly. Uniforms are compulsory in most schools, although children may have a choice of colors.

Like classrooms, public libraries are always crowded and space must be booked by the hour.

Right: Rooftop revision. Thousands of students work anywhere that is quieter than home, but this girl will still have to put up with the noise of aircraft passing above the city.

Pastimes

Sunday is most people's rest day, but it is far from peaceful, as blaring televisions compete with noisy Mah Jong games. Mah Jong, Hong Kong's national pastime, is a gambling game for four players. It is an ancient and highly skilled game that was once played with cards. Later, bamboo and ivory tiles, finely carved with Chinese characters, were used instead — nowadays the tiles are usually plastic. As the game gets more exciting, play gets faster and noisier as players shout out their moves and slam down their tiles.

A city of restaurants

Hong Kong has thousands of eating places that serve delicious, freshly cooked food. From air-conditioned restaurants to the open-air tables of the "Poor Man's Nightclub" (a daytime parking lot that is used as a market at night), rich and poor people regularly eat out at almost any time. Dining is as much a social affair as a matter of eating: the Chinese phrase "have you eaten?" can also mean "how are you." There are countless numbers of Chinese dishes and ways of cooking, for each of China's many regions has its own recipes based on local ingredients and customs. The colour and texture of a dish are

Below: People often play cards or Chinese chess in parks or open spaces. These men are playing a traditional card game for money, but they hide it from prying eyes —apart from bets on horse-racing, gambling is illegal.

An alternative is to buy shares and hope they will rise in value. People who can buy lots of shares do so at the Stock Exchange. Small amounts are sold at banks or in shopping arcades, where electronic signs flash up share prices.

Above: A crowded beach sounds like a busy market, as hoarse-voiced noodle or hamburger vendors try to shout their wares above the noise. People even take portable television sets to the beach.

For many young people, the beach is the place to meet members of the opposite sex, though they are usually introduced to each other by friends.

Below: Discussing the finer points of birds.

as important as its taste, and many dishes try to contrast flavors, such as sweet and sour pork. The Chinese are also very economical and nothing edible is wasted. Most Westerners have heard of Peking Duck, but the Chinese also consider steamed duck's feet a delicacy. *Dim sum* – delicious tiny steamed or fried dumplings with meat, fish or sweet stuffings – are only served during the day. A *dim sum* lunch on Sunday is a traditional family outing, while *yum cha* is a light snack of tea with a few *dim sum* delicacies.

Gambling fever

Hong Kong has two race courses. Both are packed on Saturdays. The races are a social event for the rich, but to many working people gambling is almost a business. Choosing a horse depends on its "form," but a horse may also have a lucky number, such as eight, which in Cantonese sounds very similar to the word for "prosperity."

Over $125,000 000 is bet on horses each year – an average of about $45.00 for each adult, and it is mainly men who gamble. The taxes raised from betting are an important source of income for the government, and it relies on them heavily. The Royal Jockey Club, which owns the race courses, spends its profits on charitable projects such as health clinics and recreation centers.

Getting away from it all

A picnic or trek on a quiet outer island is a perfect retreat from the city. Many islands are a short ferry trip from the mainland. Even Hong Kong Island has beauty spots such as Victoria Peak, which is covered with forests of pine, bamboo and ferns.

During the summer, walkers often have to line up for the most beautiful routes in the New Territories. On hot summer weekends, sandy beaches like Repulse Bay are covered with bathers trying to catch a cool breeze from the sea. The rich avoid the crowds of office and factory workers by sailing their yachts to remote beaches.

Caged birds

Caged birds are popular, especially with old men: a parakeet, canary or nightingale is an ideal pet in a tiny home. If the weather is fine, old men take their birds for a 'walk" in the open. Later, the men meet in tea houses, where special poles are provided to hang the cages from. Over a *dim sum* snack, the men swap news and discuss the birds.

Below: People gather in parks and open spaces as early as six a.m. to do traditional *Tai Chi Chuan* exercises. It's a sort of slow-motion shadow boxing that helps keep the mind and body fit, but can also be used in self defence.

Festivals

Most Hong Kong festivals celebrate the birth of a god or legendary hero. They are dazzling and noisy events, with streets full of happy people. Special food, like roast pig, fruit and colored hard-boiled eggs, is first offered to the god and then eaten by the revelers. Other festivals mark times in the traditional and ancient Chinese lunar (moon) calendar.

Most Hong Kong Chinese use two calendars – the Western solar (sun) calendar for work or appointments, and the lunar one to choose lucky dates for events like weddings or for festivals. A lunar year has 12 months unless it is a leap year, when it has 13 months. Most festivals are held on the same lunar dates – but if you are counting by the Western calendar, they will be on a different date each year. Most festivals are held during lunar months one to nine, which fall between January and September in the Western calendar.

Chinese New Year
The lunar calendar begins with Chinese New Year. This begins on day one of the first lunar month – between late January and mid February, and it lasts for 15 days. Most people get three days' vacation, and schools close for two weeks. It is a time to make peace, forget old arguments and settle debts.

New Year preparations begin 16 days before the celebration, when Chinese business owners settle their accounts for the year, and thank the gods if they have had a good year. Four days later it is time to "sweep floors clean," when men are expected to help with the spring-cleaning. People believe that later in the festival, their household kitchen god will report to heaven on their family's behavior over the past year. To make sure they get a good report, they offer rice sweets to their statue of the god. Afterwards, the children are allowed to eat the sweets.

Below: A Dragon Boat Festival race. The races are held in June. They commemorate a wise poet, who drowned himself when his king ignored the advice he had given.

A boat has a dragon's head at the bow and a dragon's tail at the stern. Some boats may be paddled by as many as 80 men. There are now races for women, though their boats are called phoenix boats.

Above: The exact date of the spring Bun Festival is decided each year by a fortune-teller. It is held on Cheung Chau island, where some people were once murdered by pirates. The festival is a way of apologizing to the dead people's ghosts.

During the four day festival, people are forbidden to eat meat or take their boats to sea. Children dress up as traditional heroes and villains, while the highlight of the festival is when pink and white lucky buns are fixed to 65 foot high bamboo towers. Until a few years ago, people raced to climb the towers and collect as many buns as possible. Accidents and fights for the highest (and luckiest) buns have caused the races to be banned. Now the buns are given away.

Right: The Festival of the Hungry Ghosts happens in the seventh lunar month. It is a time to make offerings to the spirits of the dead who have no living relatives to care for them.

On New Year's Eve the streets are full of people waiting to welcome the New Year, for they believe that this will give them a long life. On New Year's Day children "kow-tow" (bow) in respect to their parents, and people wish each other prosperity. Houses are decorated with lucky peach blossom and tiny tangerine trees. No food can be cut up with knives, for all sharp objects must be hidden in case they cut off a streak of good luck. Melon seeds, preserved fruit, fried sesame seed cakes, peanuts and molasses are special New Year food. Children are given red packets of lucky money to save or spend on sweets or toys.

The next day, people visit the temple and friends or relatives. The day after is called "squabble day," so it is a bad day for visits.

Festivals to honor the ancestors

"Clear and Bright" festival (Ching Ming) lasts ten days and marks the arrival of spring. The festival is a time for families to visit ancestral graves and tidy them up. Food and burned paper offerings are made to the dead, but it is not a sad affair, for the family will later picnic on the food. Chung Yeung is a similar festival, held in autumn. It is also known as the Kite Festival, when children are taken to fly kites in the New Territories.

Mid-Autumn Lantern festival

On the night of September's full moon thousands of people climb hills and high buildings to get a good view of the bright moon. This was originally a harvest festival, similar to Western celebrations. In the evening, families go to parks or beaches to picnic by the light of candles in paper lanterns, which are shaped like butterflies or fish, and even cars or planes.

Cakes, shaped like a full moon, are a special festival treat. Legend says that they were first made in the 14th century, and contained secret messages to the Chinese people to revolt against the foreign Mongol rulers in Peking.

Above: On the birthday of the Monkey God, a ceremony begins with a man praying until the god's spirit enters his body. Believing that he is protected by supernatural powers, the man climbs a high ladder with rungs made of sharp knives. Afterwards he runs through hot embers, feeling no pain whatsoever.

This festival happens towards the end of September. It takes place outside the Monkey God temple (in the background on the left of the picture). The temple is right in the middle of a large housing project.

33

All-weather city

Above: A television weather report during a storm.

Winds of 40 knots are reported and a force five gale warning has been issued. Typhoon Betty is 70 miles south-east of Hong Kong and its center is expected to come within 18 miles of the colony by 7 p.m. Bus and MTR services will stop in two hours' time. Employers should send their employees home as soon as possible. Warning to shipping: small vessels should head for the nearest typhoon shelter...

News bulletins like this are not unusual in summer and early autumn, when violent wind-lashed rain storms head inland from the South China Sea.

Tai Fung

The word typhoon comes from two Chinese words: *tai*, which means "big," and *fung*, which means "wind." "Big wind" is an understatement, for typhoon winds may reach 120 mph. Before computers and satellites gave early warnings, meteorologists watched the sky for typhoon signs. Today, frequent broadcasts warn people to take cover. Children are sent home from school, while shopkeepers board up doors and windows. Small boats try to shelter, but larger junks stay at sea to avoid the danger of battering against the shore or other boats. Within hours of a warning, the city seems empty.

As the typhoon closes in, the wind rises to a deafening shriek until people in high-rise apartments feel the buildings shake. People outdoors can be seriously injured by flying debris like flower pots. Towering waves whip the shore, threatening to wash people away.

Typhoons are spinning masses of air with calm centers. As the "eye" passes by there is an hour or so of peace, when stranded people can rush home. Soon the raging fury returns, demolishing shanty huts and flooding streets. Casualties can be severe, and in 1962 Typhoon Wanda killed several hundred people.

Tropical extremes

But typhoons are just an aspect of a tropical climate. Early spring hailstorms batter people and buildings with hailstones that can reach tennis ball size. From spring to summer is the monsoon season, when torrential rain can last days and wash away shanty huts and even hillside apartment blocks. At other times, Hong Kong suffers months of drought, when water must be rationed.

Summer temperatures are as high as 95°F. It is so humid that people prefer to stay indoors if they have air-conditioning. Winter temperatures can fall to freezing

Above: Hong Kong's weather encourages tropical plants and flowers like azeleas, orchids and bamboo. Pine, Chinese fir and acacia trees grow on the cooler hills.

Getting around

Because Hong Kong is so hilly, people seldom travel in a straight line from one place to another. Apart from Hong Kong Island, the colony's 235 islands can only be reached by boat. For example, someone from Yuen Long in the New Territories, needs at least one bus and two ferry trips to go for a swim on Lamma Island. But because millions of people use it, public transport is efficient and fares are fairly low.

"Wallah-wallahs" and ferries

In the past, small sailing junks and sampans, "wallah-wallahs," were the only way to reach the islands. Since the first steam ferry began in 1870, more and more ferries have linked up the islands. Today, double-decker green and white "Star Ferries" are a common sight and make hundreds of daily trips, taking commuters back and forth from the main island to Kowloon. People can enjoy a trip on a motor "wallah-wallah," and although they are much more expensive, they are useful when the Mass Transit Railway and ferries close down at night.

Red or blue buses

Two private companies run frequent bus

Right: At rush hours up to 150 people squeeze on one of the streetcars that clank and rumble down the lines on the north of Hong Kong Island. They are the main way to get around for the 1,500,000 people who live on the island. All trams are covered in bright advertisements. This one has a government message: "Serve people politely and help them honestly."

Below: For its size, Hong Kong has an astonishing number of vehicles. Tunnels have been bored into hills so that roads no longer have to follow the valleys around the hill. To prevent traffic jams, new junctions and overpasses are always under construction. The latest is an 8.2 m road built on stilts over the sea, on the north side of Hong Kong Island.

Above: A car on the Mass Transit Railway, which links Kowloon and Hong Kong Island to parts of the New Territories. The MTR is the fastest way to get around, but it costs more than buses or streetcars, so fewer people use it.

The main line from Hong Kong to China is also used as a local train. Police who check visas at the border make sure that nobody ends up in China by mistake.

Left: A Star Ferry Company boat crosses between Kowloon and Hong Kong Island. The Central Business District offices of Hong Kong Island can be seen in the background.

This is the cheapest way to cross the harbor, and takes about eight minutes. Passengers who get seasick prefer the upper first-class decks, where there is more fresh air.

Motorists use the cross-harbor tunnel, or take a half-hour trip on the car ferry.

services that reach even the most remote New Territories villages. *Kowloon Motor Buses* are painted red, while *China Motor Buses* are blue. Recently, "mini-buses," seating 14 people, have bridged the gap between expensive taxis and cheap buses. They pick up passengers anywhere on the route, and charge according to the length of a journey and the number of people sharing the taxi.

A cable railway and the rickshaw "boys"

The Peak Tram, a 19th century cable railway, rises over 400 metres up a very steep incline to the top of Victoria Peak. Commuters once used it, but today cheaper mini-buses have left it mainly to the tourists to enjoy the scenery and views of the harbor.

Just after World War II, over 8,000 men made a living pulling passengers in two-wheeled carts. These rickshaw "boys" tended to ignore road signs and were a traffic hazard, so the government is not issuing any more licences. Today, only a few aging "boys" survive, carrying rich tourists and charging them to photograph their quaint rickshaws.

Many years ago, rich people avoided Hong Kong's filthy streets by traveling in sedan chairs carried by two or four coolies. Today the sedan chairs are gone forever, but traditional donkey and bullock carts are still found in the New Territories, though even these are rapidly being replaced by trucks and bicycles.

Gateway to China

Below: The container port at Kwai Chung is the third largest in the world, and has very efficient methods of handling freight. Hong Kong is famous for its shipbuilding, and some of the world's richest shipowners live there.

Hong Kong may be ruled by Britain, but its position makes it one of the most important gateways to China.

Hong Kong's trade with China is more important than ever. But though 19th century English merchants in Hong Kong once sold opium to China, China now sells billions of dollars' worth of goods to Hong Kong each year. The colony relies on China for much of its food, and even fresh water.

Every day cargo trains rumble across the border from China, carrying pigs, poultry, vegetables and fruit to the city. Freight cars full of pigs are followed by swarms of flies and mosquitoes that sometimes invade nearby apartments.

Soon Hong Kong will even buy electricity from a nearby Chinese nuclear power station.

China needs Western money

As well as feeding Hong Kong, China sends a large part of its exports to the West through Hong Kong's ports. The colony is very important to China as a place to earn Western money, because plans for China's modernization need sophisticated Western machinery, which can only be paid for with Western money. So companies run by the Chinese government in Hong Kong use profits from making things like heavy machinery, cement and beer to buy foreign equipment, which is then shipped to China. When property prices rose rapidly in the 1970s, several Chinese companies bought land from the Hong Kong government. Later, they built offices and luxury apartments to rent or sell for huge profits.

Right: Coming in to land at Hong Kong's busy Kai Tak airport in Kowloon. Planes land so close to the built-up areas that their passengers can see people eating, through the windows of high-rise apartments.

The whole of the airport runway is built on reclaimed land. Flat building land is a rare and precious commodity in Hong Kong. Much of the shore land of Hong Kong Island and Kowloon was once sea, that has been filled in with rubble. The rubble often comes from hillsides that have been dug out and flattened for more buildings.

Below: A live pig, painted with red identification marks, is unloaded onto a Hong Kong quayside. Pork is a very important part of a Chinese diet, and most of it comes from Chinese pigs imported by rail or sea.

Traditional Chinese packaging is made by hand from natural materials such as palm branches, split bamboo or strong leaves. Such containers have been used to transport almost anything – from bags of cement to a fragile egg.

Hong Kong needs China

It's a two-way trade, for many business people realize that part of Hong Kong's success depends on China. Many European, American and Japanese companies have Hong Kong offices, through which they hope to sell their services and products to China, for they know that China wants to buy many things that it cannot produce for itself. And, because labor is cheaper in China than in Hong Kong, some Hong Kong businesses have set up factories across the border, which make handbags and jeans for overseas sale.

A tourist gateway

Tourists who visit China usually start off from Hong Kong. The easiest way is to go on a tour arranged by travel agents who specialize in China. China has few Western-style hotels, but for the more adventurous, it is possible to travel alone in China. In return, tourists from China began to visit Hong Kong in 1983, the first time that this has been allowed since 1949.

China watchers

Until recently, few visitors got into China, and very little accurate news came out. The rest of the world was eager to know what was going on, so Hong Kong became a post for "China-watchers" – specialists and journalists who sifted through every clue about the mysterious country. Today their task is less important, for China welcomes visitors and provides much more information about its affairs.

Right: Lo Wu station on the border with Hong Kong and China. There are two daily nonstop expresses to China, but Hong Kong people who visit relatives just over the border take a stopping train to Lo Wu, and then change to a local Chinese train. Trains are full of people taking refrigerators, televison sets, radios or cameras to their relatives. They often return with food, which is cheaper to buy in China. The border is extremely busy at Chinese New Year.

A place on borrowed time

Hong Kong lives on time borrowed from China. The 99 year lease on the New Territories runs out in 1997. (Hong Kong Island and Kowloon were granted to Britain forever, but they could not survive without the resources of the New Territories.)

Hong Kong, China

Until recently the British government, like most people in Hong Kong, hoped that somehow it could continue to run the colony after 1997. But Britain has had to accept the fact that China will not extend the lease. In 1984 the two countries agreed that after July 1, 1997 the colony would become part of China. However, it will not be run in the same way as the rest of China for another 50 years. The colony will be allowed to keep its lifestyle and laws almost unchanged until 2047.

Doubts for the future?

Despite China's promises, nobody really knows what Hong Kong will be like under Chinese rule. The Chinese government might change its mind about the way it wants to run Hong Kong. People worry that they may have to serve in the Chinese army, or that they may

Above: At the beginning of 1984 taxi drivers gathered to protest against the government's plans to increase license fees. Soon they were joined by other people, who turned the protest into a riot and an opportunity to show their anger and frustration at their lack of involvement in the way Hong Kong is run.

Right: Lo Wu, the border between China and Hong Kong. By 1997 the British Union Jack will be taken down, and eventually there will be no need for a border between Hong Kong and China.

find it difficult to follow their religions. Business owners do not know if they will be able to continue to make profits for themselves, and this lack of confidence discourages people from investing money in Hong Kong factories. That could lead to fewer jobs and unemployment.

An outdated colonial rule

Discussions about Hong Kong's future have reminded people how little they can influence their own future. Britain has always chosen the governor of Hong Kong from London. The governor appoints a small group of people to help him run the colony. Ordinary people have almost no say in the government of their country. The only people for whom they can vote are a few minor officials, who control such things as parks or museums, and issue traders' licenses.

Many older immigrants still accept the traditional Chinese teachings and customs, which do not encourage people to challenge authority. The generation that left China for Hong Kong contents itself with trying to earn a living. But they are now outnumbered by younger people, who were born and bred in the colony and who are no longer prepared to accept the old ways.

Many young people resent their lack of influence, especially if they can see no escape from the poverty of crowded slums or shanty towns. Occasionally their discontentment has exploded into anger on the streets, where buses have been stoned, shops looted, cars set afire, and Westerners jeered at.

During the course of the last ten years or so the government has tried to involve Hong Kong people in the running of the colony, by employing more Chinese in the Civil Service. Nevertheless, most senior posts are still held by Europeans, and Chinese people are sometimes paid less than Europeans for doing similar jobs.

Packing up to leave?

Hong Kong already plays an important part in China's plans for modernization. The terms of the agreement between Britain and China should ensure that China continues to earn Western money from Hong Kong.

Despite this reassurance, some wealthier people will inevitably abandon Hong Kong: some companies have already moved their headquarters out to other countries. But the vast majority of people will not be able to afford this choice. They have coped with major changes in the past, and they will have to do so again in the future. After all, most of Hong Kong's population is Chinese and, whatever people may feel about Communist rule, it will be Chinese rule.

Above: Shenzhen, a new town in China, just over the Hong Kong border. China gives financial aid to foreign businesses which open factories here, where taxes and wages are lower than in Hong Kong. In return, the factories help China to earn Western money and gain experience to run modern factories in other parts of China.

Such cooperation between China and the West could smooth the way to Chinese rule over Hong Kong.

Right: Mrs. Brenca Chau poses by her Rolls Royce cars. People like the Chaus can afford to start a new life if they do not want to live in Hong Kong ruled by China.

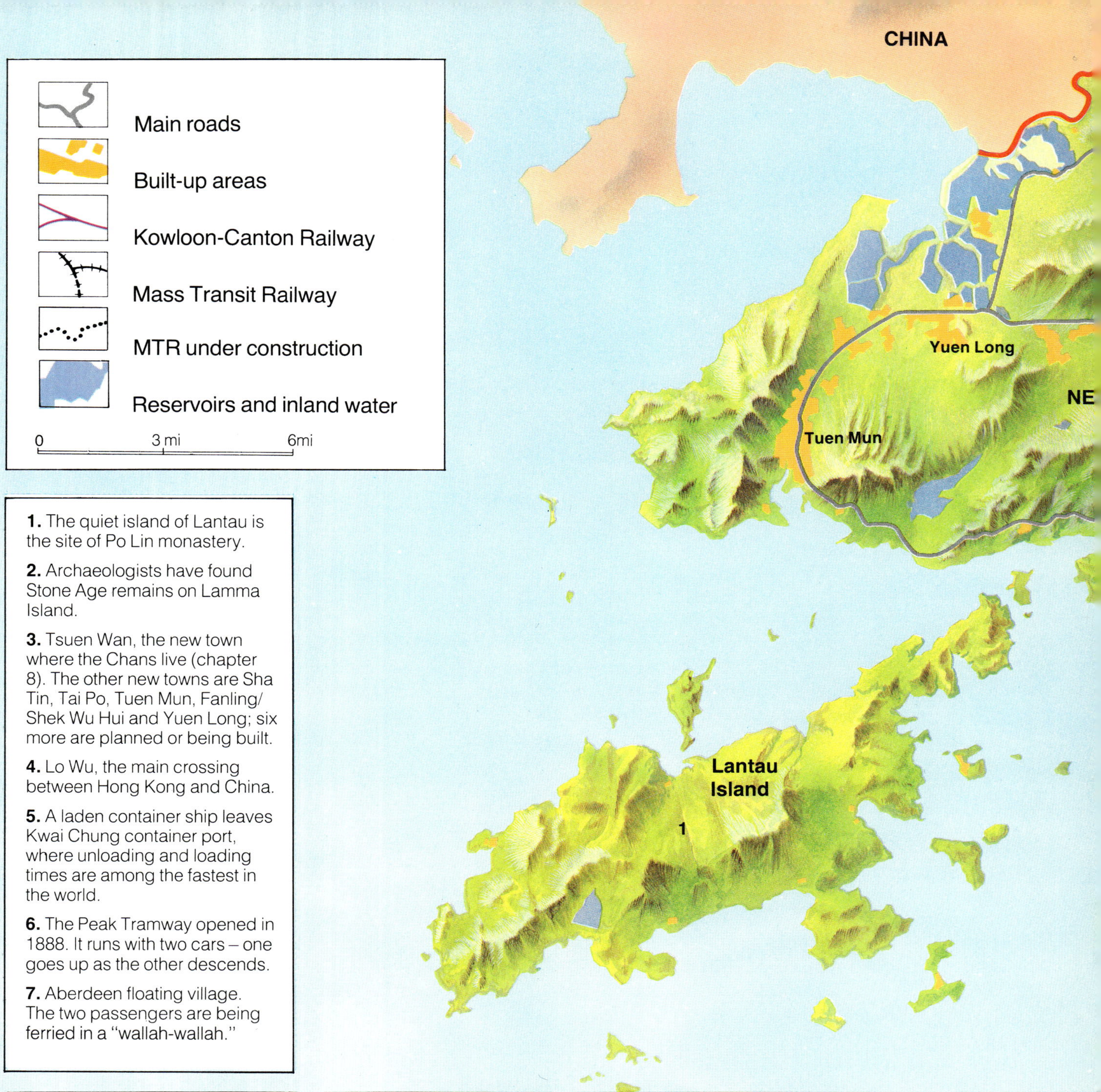

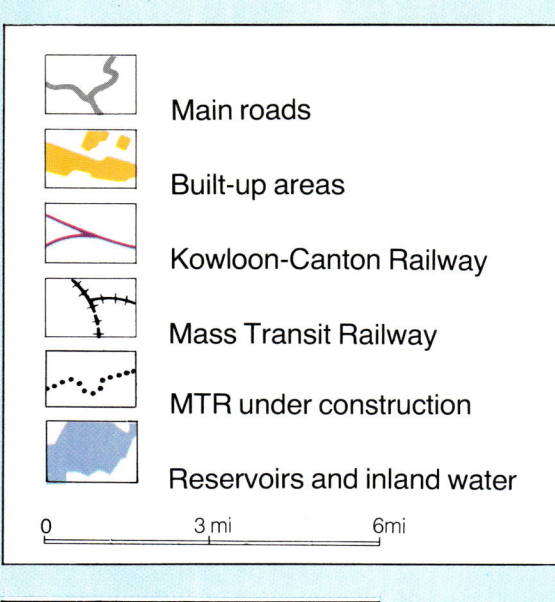

Legend:
- Main roads
- Built-up areas
- Kowloon-Canton Railway
- Mass Transit Railway
- MTR under construction
- Reservoirs and inland water

0   3 mi   6 mi

CHINA

Yuen Long

Tuen Mun

NE

Lantau Island

1. The quiet island of Lantau is the site of Po Lin monastery.

2. Archaeologists have found Stone Age remains on Lamma Island.

3. Tsuen Wan, the new town where the Chans live (chapter 8). The other new towns are Sha Tin, Tai Po, Tuen Mun, Fanling/Shek Wu Hui and Yuen Long; six more are planned or being built.

4. Lo Wu, the main crossing between Hong Kong and China.

5. A laden container ship leaves Kwai Chung container port, where unloading and loading times are among the fastest in the world.

6. The Peak Tramway opened in 1888. It runs with two cars — one goes up as the other descends.

7. Aberdeen floating village. The two passengers are being ferried in a "wallah-wallah."

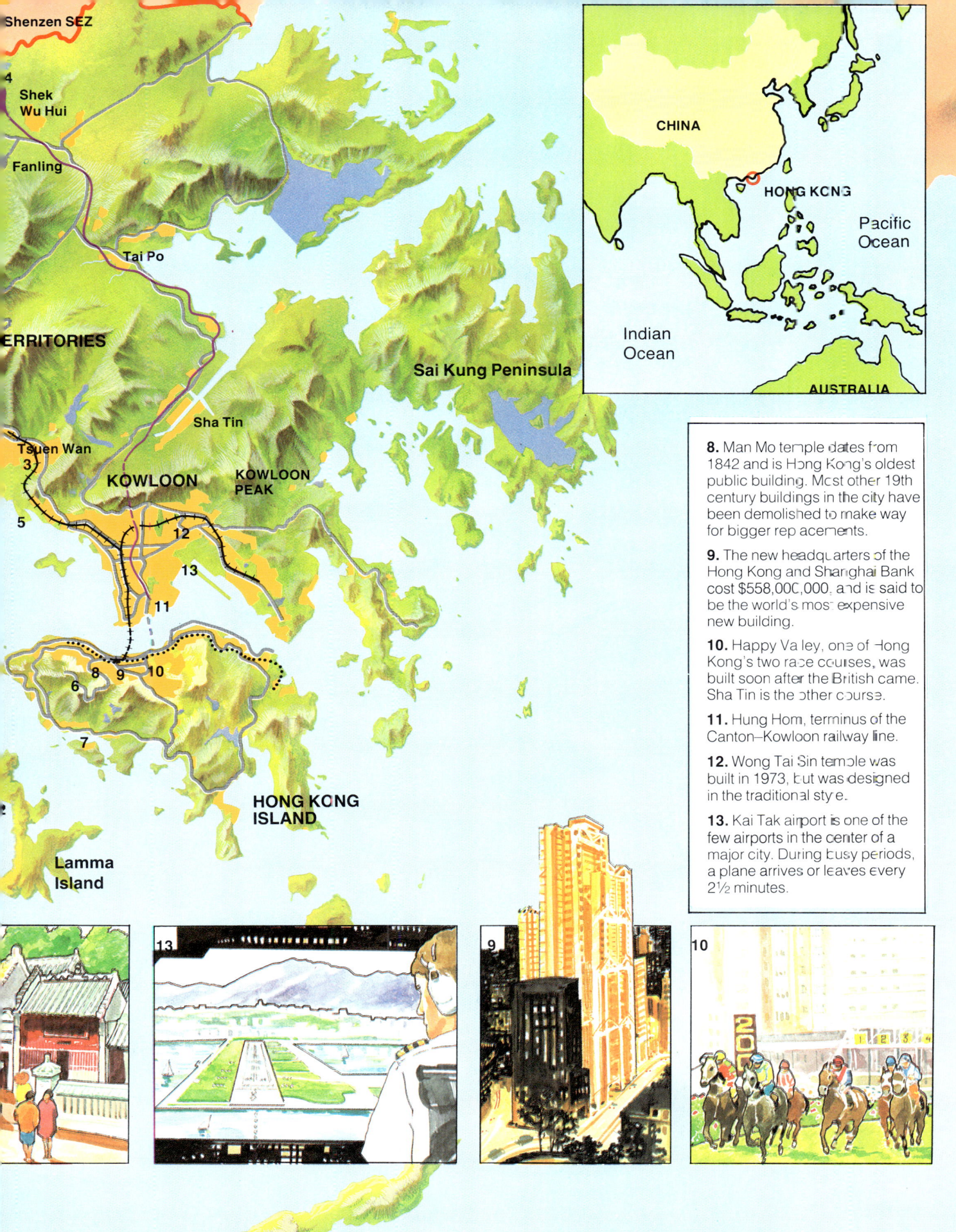

8. Man Mo temple dates from 1842 and is Hong Kong's oldest public building. Most other 19th century buildings in the city have been demolished to make way for bigger replacements.

9. The new headquarters of the Hong Kong and Shanghai Bank cost $558,000,000, and is said to be the world's most expensive new building.

10. Happy Valley, one of Hong Kong's two race courses, was built soon after the British came. Sha Tin is the other course.

11. Hung Hom, terminus of the Canton–Kowloon railway line.

12. Wong Tai Sin temple was built in 1973, but was designed in the traditional style.

13. Kai Tak airport is one of the few airports in the center of a major city. During busy periods, a plane arrives or leaves every 2½ minutes.

The Chinese lunar calendar

For thousands of years China has used a lunar calendar, which marks time by the moon's orbits round the earth. Each month begins on a new moon, and there are 12 months to a year. Today most people mark time by the earth's orbits round the sun (solar calendar), giving the familiar months January to December. Lunar months are a day or two shorter than solar months, so every two or three years an extra month is added to a lunar year to keep it in pace with the solar calendar.

Originally, the lunar calendar helped farmers to plan their work. Each month is divided into two parts, which have names like "white dew" or "grain in the beard." The lunar calendar is still used by people in Hong Kong to mark the many Chinese festivals.

Right: A chart of the animals of the Chinese calendar, which people use to tell their fortunes. It is a similar system to Western signs of the zodiac.

Each lunar year is named after one of 12 animals, which always follow each other in the same order. (For example, Pig follows Dog.) People tell their fortune according to the personality of the animal of their birth year. Many Chinese people take their animal signs very seriously. The short descriptions in this chart are highly simplified. A professional horoscope is much more detailed, and uses an individual's precise time of birth.

1950
1962
1974
1986

Tiger Years: Tiger people are thoughtful and make faithful friends; they also make dangerous enemies. They are brave people who are respected by others, but they can be mistrustful and selfish.

1951
1963
1975
1987

Rabbit Years: Rabbit people are gifted and lucky and have excellent taste. Patient and shy, these people do not easily lose their tempers. Rabbit people are smooth talkers who are trusted by others.

1952
1964
1976
1988

Dragon Years: Dragon people are healthy, brave and energetic. Though emotional and short-tempered, they are born leaders. Dragon people worry a lot and tend to talk too much.

1948
1960
1972
1984

Rat Years: Rat people born at night are brave, but cautious if born in the day. They are charming, but quick to anger. Rat people are thrifty, persistent and ambitious: they enjoy gossip.

1949
1961
1973
1985

Ox Years: Ox people are trustworthy; although they are calm and quiet, they can be stubborn. They are clever with their hands and, if born during the day, particularly lucky. They are often hard workers.

1953
1965
1977
1989
Snake Years: Snake people are very likely to become rich (they are often mean with money). Wise and enthusiastic, such people are popular with others but can be conceited and unfaithful.

1954
1966
1978
1990
Horse Years: Horse people are intelligent and independent, and are liked by other people. They are cheerfully talkative, but careful with money. They tend to fall hopelessly in love.

1955
1967
1979
1991

Ram Years: Ram people are very artistic and often use their skills to make money. They can be mild-mannered and very caring, but they can also be harsh or cruel. They are often indecisive.

1956
1968
1980
1992

Monkey Years: Monkey people are clever and very creative – success comes easily to them. They also have a reputation for being disrespectful trouble-makers, who scheme to get their own way.

1957
1969
1981
1993

Rooster Years: Rooster people can be humble, but also arrogant. They are often loners who have great plans that may come to nothing. Rooster people work hard, but they are not careful with money.

1958
1970
1982
1994
Dog Years: Dog people are loyal, hard-working and trustworthy; they command great respect in others. They hate injustice and may be headstrong, and are sometimes confused and erratic in their actions.

1959
1971
1983
1995

Pig Years: Pig people are very brave and determined. They are very close to friends and loved ones, but they do not find friendship easily. They study hard at subjects that they are interested in.

The Chinese language

There is no Chinese alphabet. Instead of words, Chinese is written in signs called characters. One character can express the meaning of a whole phrase in a language that uses words. Some characters still resemble the ancient picture signs from which they were developed. The large character below represents "root;" it also describes books, the "root of knowledge." Many systems exist to write Chinese using a Western alphabet. The most familiar of these (Wade-Giles) has been used throughout this book: China now uses a different system called Pin-yin. An example is "Peking" (Wade-Giles) and "Beijing" (Pin-yin).

The Chinese character for "root" (left) is based on the outline of a tree. Without the bottom cross bar, it would mean "wood." The two words (below) show how the "root" character can be used to convey new meanings.

(本國) my country   本子 notebook

Index

Numbers in heavy type refer to picture captions, or to the pictures themselves.

America 10, 26, 39
ancestors and ancestor worship 12, **12**, 16, **16**, 17, **25**, **32**, 33, **33**

beliefs **15**
(see also fortune-tellers, *fung-shui*, religion)
boat cover, **6**, 9, 10, 18, 20, **20**, 21, **21**, **32**, **33**, 34, 36, **36**, **37**, **38**, **42**, **43**
British 8, 10, **10**, 28, **29**, 38, 40, **40**, 41, **43**
Buddhism 13, 14, **19**

calendars 32, 44
Cantonese 8, 9, 10, 16, 17
cemeteries **12**, 13
China 8, 9, 10, 11, 14, 17, **17**, 20, 21, 28, **37**, 38, 39, **39**, 40, **40**, 41, **41**, **42**, **43**
Chinese 8, 9, 10, 11, 12, **12**, 13, 14, **16**, 17, **19**, 27, 28, **29**, 30, **30**, 31, 32, 33, **39**, 41, 44
Christians 15, 19
clans 9, 16, 17, 28
climate 10, **22**, 23, 24, 34, **34**, 35, **35**
clothes 16, **17**
computers (see technology)
Confucius 12
coolies 10, 37
crafts 18, **26**, 27
customs 8, 9, 12, **12**, 13, **13**, 16, **17**, 18, 20, 28, **28**, 30, 31, 32, **32**, 33, **33**, 41
(see also religion)

disease 10

education (see schools, universities)
electricity 18, 21, 22, 23, **23**, 38
English (see British)
Europeans 8, 10, 39, 41
(see also British)

families 12
farmers 15, **16**, 17, **17**
feetbinding 9
festivals 14, **16**, **29**, 32, **32**, 33, **33**, 44
Filipinos 8
fish **16**, 20, **20**, 21
fisherfolk and fishing cover, **6**, 9, 14, **18**, 20, **20**, 21, **21**
floating villages cover, **6**, 9, 20, **20**, 21, **21**, **42**, **43**
food 14, **16**, 17, 18, **19**, 20, **20**, 21, **21**, 24, **24**, **25**, 30, 31, 32, **32**, 33, **33**, 38, **39**
fortune-tellers 12, **15**, **15**, **33**, 44
funerals 12
fung-shui 12, 13, **13**, 14

Hakka 9, **9**, 16, 17, **17**
Hoklo 9, 20
homes and housing cover, **6**, 8, **8**, 9, 10, 17, 19, 20, **20**, 21, **21**, 22, **22**, 23, **23**, 24, **24**, 25, **25**, 26, 35, 38, **38**, 41

immigrants 9, **10**, 21, 41
Indians 8, 27
industry 11, 16, 17, 19, **24**, 26, **26**, 27, **27**, 33, **38**, 39, **42**, **43**
(see also work)
islands 8, 16, 18, **18**, 19, 36, **42**, **43**

Japan 11, 39
Jews 15

Korea (North and South) 11
Kowloon 8, **11**, 16, 19, 27, 36, **37**, **38**, 40

language 9, 28, **29**, 44
Lantau 18, 19, **19**, **20**, 42
leisure 5, **6**, **7**, 17, **19**, 21, 24, **24**, **25**, 28, **28**, 30, **30**, 31, **31**, **43**

market **16**, 30
(see also shops)
Mass Transit Railway 13, 16, 36, **37**, **42**, **43**
Muslims 15

New Territories 8, 9, 10, 16, **16**, 17, 24, **24**, 25, 28, 31, 33, 36, 37, **37**, 40
New Year (Chinese) 32, 33, **39**

opium 10, **10**, 38

pastimes (see leisure)
peoples 8, 9, 11, 15, 18, **18**, 20, 27
Christians 15, 19
Filipinos 8
Hoklo 9, 20
Indians 8, 27
Jews 15
Muslims 15
Sikhs 15
Tanka 9, 20
(see also Chinese, Hakka)
population (see peoples)
poverty 9, 10, 22, 23, 27, 28, 30, 41
prehistory **18**, **42**
protest **40**, 41

refugees 10, 11, 17
religion 12, 14, **14**, 15, **15**, 16, **16**, 17, 18, 19, **19**, 32, **32**, 33, **33**, 41, **42**, **43**

schools 21, 25, **27**, 28, **29**
shanty towns (see squatters)
ships (see boats)
shops 21, 26, 27
(see also markets)
Sikhs 15
sports 5, **6**, 28, 31, **31**, **43**
(see also leisure)
squatters 22, **22**, 23, **23**

Tai Chi Chuan exercises **31**
Tanka 9, 20
Taoism 14
technology **26**, 27, **27**, 34, 38
temples 8, 14, **14**, 15, **15**, 17, 19, **43**
tourists **17**, 19, **20**, 21, 27, 37, 39
trade 8, 10, 11, 17, 26, 27, 38, 39, **39**
traditions (see customs)
transport 8, 9, 13, 16, 18, 19, 36, **36**, 37, **37**, 38, **38**, 39, **39**, **42**, **43**
typhoons **22**, 23, 34, 35

universities 28

Vietnam 13
villages cover, **6**, 8, 9, 12, 13, 15, 16, 17, 20, **20**, 21, **21**, **42**, **43**
(see also homes)

wars 10, 11
water supplies 16, **17**, 18, 21, **21**, 22, 23, 35, 38
wealth 11, 13, 27, 30, **30**, 31, **38**, 41, **41**
weather (see climate)
weddings 12, 13
work **6**, 9, **9**, 10, 11, 14, 16, **16**, 17, **17**, 18, **18**, 19, 20, 21, **23**, 25, 26, **26**, 27, **27**, 28, **29**, 41
(see also industry)